Old TROON

by

Ian MacPherson

CW00944255

THE STATION TROON.

Troon's first railway station stood on Dundonald Road and was opened on the main Ayr to Glasgow line in 1840. It was replaced in May 1892 by the present station (pictured) which was opened on a loop line some two and a quarter miles long, bringing the railway into the centre of a rapidly growing village. The covered canopy bridge built by Alex Findlay & Co. was removed during the station's renovation of 1985-87 to allow for electrification of the line. Engine no. 224 belonged to the Glasgow & South Western Railway Company who operated the line until 1923.

© Ian MacPherson, 2000
First published in the United Kingdom, 2000,
by Stenlake Publishing
01290 551122
www.stenlake.co.uk
ISBN 978-1-84033-101-1

THE PUBLISHERS REGRET THAT THEY CANNOT SUPPLY
COPIES OF ANY PICTURES FEATURED IN THIS BOOK.

ACKNOWLEDGEMENTS

The author wishes to thank Robert Gemmell for his research on the churches
of Troon and for assistance with other information. The publishers wish to
thank Sandy Crawford of Crawford's of Ayr for permission to reproduce the
pictures on page 38 and the back cover, and Robert Grieves for the picture
on the inside front cover.

FURTHER READING

The books listed below were used by the author during his research. None
of them are available from Stenlake Publishing. Those interested in finding
out more are advised to contact their local bookshop or reference library.

Douglas Cotter & Alan Stewart, *Purple & Gold: The Story of Marr College and
    the C.K. Marr Educational Trust*, 1996.
Rev. J.H. Gillespie, *Dundonald, the Parish and its Setting*, 1939.
John Keay & Julia Keay, *Collins Encyclodpedia of Scotland*, 1994.
Rev. J. Kirkwood, *Troon and Dundonald*, 1876.
Ian M. Mackintosh, *Old Troon & District*, 1969.
Ian M. Mackintosh, *Memories of Old Troon*, 1972.
John Strawhorn & William Boyd, *Third Statistical Account – Ayrshire*, 1951.
History of Portland Parish Church – 1843-1993.

Scotia Sea in the South Atlantic is named after the *Scotia*, pictured here in
Troon Harbour. Powered by sail and steam, the ship was built as a whaler but
was refitted at the Ailsa yard in order to carry the Scottish National Antarctic
Expedition which sailed from Troon in 1902, returning in 1904. (This
expedition is not to be confused with the more famous National Antarctic
Expedition which sailed in 1901 under the command of Captain Scott.) The
trip was financed by Andrew Coats of Paisley, the thread manufacturers,
and commanded by the naturalist, Dr William Spiers Bruce. The ship was
captained by Thomas Robertson of Dundee.

INTRODUCTION

At the close of the eighteenth century Troon was a clachan of around 200 people engaged mainly in fishing, salt-making, and the popular pastime of smuggling contraband *via* the Isle of Man. The existence of a ridge of rocks running seawards for a distance of almost a mile made it well-known to seafarers as a fairly secure anchorage in the prevailing south westerly gales. It had no school or church which were prerequisites for the status of parish and thus the clachan was merely the western extremity of the Parish of Dundonald and Crosbie.

In reference to the rocks, the name 'Troon' is derived either from the Gaelic *an-Trone*, meaning 'the nose' or 'the bill', or from the Cymric *trwyn* or *trone*, the Welsh for 'nose'. Both Low St Meddans and High St Meddans were districts in Troon and this name is probably derived from a bishop called St Meddinus or St Mirren. A chapel dedicated to him is situated in Paisley Abbey which was founded by one Walter Fitz Allan, the first High Steward of Scotland and one of the earliest proprietors of the Dundonald area. In 1608 the Royal Burgh of Irvine was given permission to erect a new harbour 'callit the Trone' and in 1707 the Fullarton family was granted a charter constituting the Port of Troon as a free seaport and harbour, which allowed it to extract a levy from all vessels landing or loading materials.

The Fullartons had been in possession of Fullarton Estate for some centuries when in 1745 the father of the last owner, Colonel William Fullarton, had a new mansion house built to replace the fortalice of Crosbie which stood in the woods close by. By 1805 Col. Fullarton was running low in funds which had gone towards raising regiments for the Napoleonic Wars and the estate was sold to William Henry Bentinck, Marquis of Titchfield. He became the fourth Duke of Portland in 1809 on the death of his father, William Cavendish Bentinck, who had been Prime Minister twice in 1783 and again from 1807 to 1809. It was largely due to the efforts of the Duke that the town entered a period of rapid development that lasted throughout the nineteenth century, culminating in the award of Burgh status in October 1896.

Through marriage the Duke gained estates in Kilmarnock, including coal mines, and in 1807 he drew up plans for a 'Rail Way' to run the ten miles between the two towns as an economical means of shipping his coal to Ireland or along the west coast. Scotland's first Rail Way was completed in 1811 and initially the wagons were horse-drawn, although a steam locomotive called 'The Duke' was bought in 1817. Unfortunately, its weight broke the cast iron rails and it had to be withdrawn until its iron wheels had been replaced with wooden ones. Passengers were also carried on the line in 'Caledonias' which resembled the modern tramcar and were built at Dundonald.

The trade in coal also led to the development of Troon's harbour and construction of a 500 foot quay, running at right angles to the rocks, began in 1808. A shipbuilding yard was opened in 1815 and by 1840 a longer breakwater had been built to protect the outer harbour which led into a wet dock excavated out of solid rock, two dry docks and an inner harbour. The availability of work at the harbour and on the Rail Way soon caused a rapid growth in the population and huts were erected for accommodation.

Before long congregations were established and churches built, and education was also made available in Troon long before it became compulsory in 1877. Mrs Stevenson ran a school in a cottage to the rear of the present Unionist Buildings and there was also Darley School which was built between Troon and Loans not far from the junction of Wilson Avenue and Dundonald Road. Troon Academy was built in 1840. Its first roll had fifty names but this had increased to 180 by 1875 when Portland Public School was opened on the opposite side of Academy Street (remaining as the infant school until 1963). Troon Fullarton Public School was built in Barassie Street in 1900 to cater for 800 pupils and by 1908 an extension was added to deal with increasing numbers and the name was changed to Troon Higher Grade School. Marr College, an amazing achievement for the town realised through the generosity of a local industrialist, opened in 1935 and the constant growth of housing in the Burgh since then brought new primary schools at Muirhead in 1964 and at Barassie in 1970.

Even before the shipbuilding and coal mining industries began to decline, the benefits of sea bathing at Troon were attracting visitors who were quick to appreciate the town's natural assets: two fine sandy beaches which shelved gradually into the water to permit safe bathing. Links golf courses were available at either end of the town and three municipal courses were conveniently accessible from the railway station. Summer visitors who had enjoyed the amenities and the varied choice of shops sometimes chose to take up permanent residence, and to this day Troon continues to attract incomers who want to live by the coast and also to take advantage of the convenient road and rail links with Glasgow, Kilmarnock, Irvine, Prestwick and Ayr.

TROON FROM THE STATION LOOKING NORTH.

Barassie Street from the Station. All that remains of the greenhouses and market garden on the left is the building that was the shop. In 1822 the Seceders built a church on the south side of this road just before the bridge. This building was later used at different times by the town's Established, Free and United Presbyterian churches and may well have been used as a school on weekdays. By the 1890s it had become a fever hospital and then the Burgh Buildings where the Police Court was held until 1932 when the Municipal Buildings were opened. Thereafter, it was converted to flats and finally became a store until its demolition in 1990.

BARASSIE ST. & STATION, TROON.

Barassie Street, looking south to the station from a point between Troon Higher Grade School and the Troon Co-operative Dairy (now the site of the Safeway supermarket). The building on the left at the corner of Burnside Place has the legend 'The Tinnion Nursing Home' above the doorway and for a time was used as a nurses' home and had clinic next door.

PORTLAND STREET, TROON

The obvious landmarks in this 1923 view of Portland Street are White's Newsagents (now W.H. Smith) and the Picture House (now occupied by Woolworth's) which was owned by Troon Picture House Ltd and had 850 seats. It had competition from the town's other cinemas, the George and the Pavilion, and closed in the early 1950s when the property was sold to Woolworth's. Portland Street Free Church stood in this area from 1856 until it was demolished around 1926, although worship stopped in 1914.

The Cross and Portland Street, *c.* 1907. The railway bridge to the north carried goods traffic from the new railway station to the harbour and was removed in 1973. The four storey building on the right was erected in 1902-03. In 1871 the town's lifeboat station was also built on this street. The first crew had been formed the previous year and for years sailing or rowing boats were used until a motor boat was acquired in 1929.

The Unionist Club buildings at the foot of Templehill were built in 1894 and also provided new premises for the Union Bank of Scotland which was previously situated at the top of Templehill (this bank amalgamated with the Bank of Scotland in 1955). The large suite of halls on the upper floor has now been converted to maisonettes. On the left is an ice cream barrow and note the unusual drinking fountain which has been incorporated in the gas mantle lamp-post.

The view of the Cross from Templehill to Ayr Street has little changed over the last century. The four storey property on the left replaced an earlier two storey building which included Cunningham's pub. The steeple is that of the new Established Church (later Troon Old Parish) which opened in May 1838. The Ailsa Bar was replaced by the still resplendent Tog's Cafe whose ice cream has been savoured by many visitors. The business was established by Giovanni Togneri following his arrival from Tuscany around the turn of the twentieth century. His first cafe was in a purpose built wooden building two doors up from the Ailsa, but this burned down and the business moved to the site of the Ailsa in 1914. The original green and black vitrolite fixtures from the 1914 counter still survive while the current shop front was put in during a 1950s renovation.

The houses on Templehill were built around 1845 and it was on the higher ground behind them that Colonel Fullarton had earlier built a small octagonal summer house which had views over both bays. Locals called it 'Fullarton's Folly' or the 'Temple', which probably accounts for the area's name. On the extreme right of this view are the original premises of the Union Bank of Scotland and beside it the Portland Arms Hotel, now the Anchorage Hotel. This was granted its license in 1816 and passengers were brought here by carriage from Troon's first railway station.

HARBOUR, TROON.

The harbour viewed from the top of Templehill in the vicinity of the terminus of the railway line. Behind the loaded wagons lies the Inner Basin, now dredged for the Marina, with the shipyard beyond. Note the logging area at the head of the basin where wood was stored for the sawmill sited near the present Marina office. This was established in 1870 and is still in business. Troon's earliest industry, apart from fishing, was salt-making which was carried out at the Pan Rocks on the north shore until the repeal of the salt tax and the influx of cheaper salt from England in the early 1800s. In his history of the town from the 1870s, Rev. Kirkwood notes that there were still inhabitants around at that time who could remember the boiling pans and also the occasion when an unfortunate workman, John Campbell, fell into one and was killed.

Troon Tug and "Arranmore" in Troon Harbour

The steam-powered tug *Troon* moored outside the Wet Dock in the outer harbour with the *Arranmore* awaiting cargo at the other quay, which from 1903 was used by the West of Scotland Shipbreaking Co. Ltd. Shipbuilding began in Troon when the Duke of Portland opened his yard in 1810 and in 1843 this was leased to the Troon Shipbuilding Company. By 1885 the Ailsa Shipbuilding Company had taken over, although the Duke sold the harbour to the Glasgow & South Western Railway Company in 1901. Ailsa is still in business today, constructing small craft.

A loaded coal wagon about to be emptied into the hold of the *Eros* in the Wet Dock, 1905. Coal had been essential to the local economy since 1810 when the Duke of Portland opened his Rail Way from Kilmarnock to Troon and by the 1930s over three million tons were passing through the ports of Troon, Ayr, Irvine and Ardrossan combined. The industry went into decline from the 1950s and thereafter shipments from all the Ayrshire harbours dropped.

Passengers boarding the S.S. *Juno*. This paddle steamer was built in 1898 by Barclay Curle & Co. Ltd of Clydebank for the Glasgow & South Western Railway Company and based at Ayr for sailings to Arran.

S.S. "Juno" in
Troon Harbour

The *Juno* at the pierhead just inside the entrance to the harbour, *c.* 1911. During the First World War the ship was requisitioned for war use and was stationed in the Firths of Clyde and Forth as a minesweeper. She remained in service until 1931 and was sold and broken up the following year.

A Royal Navy torpedo squadron, dressed overall in Troon Harbour around 1908. The ship in the foreground is H.M.S. *Moy* which was built in 1904 and the squadron was likely to have been based at Stranraer.

"THE PIERROTS" TROON.

'Dad Lindsay's Pierrots' performing at the south end of the Ballast Bank. The absence of the Harbour Housing Scheme enables a view of the coal wagons on the harbour railway and the shipbuilding yard behind. The Ballast Bank is a man-made mound which was probably started around 1840, initially using excavated rock from the creation of the Wet Dock. It provides the harbour area with protection from the sea and as the name suggests it also probably contains ballast from the ships that came to load up with coal or wood.

The same troop, *c.* 1910. The houses of Welbeck Crescent (named after estates owned by the Duke of Portland in England) can be seen at the top and to the extreme left is Portland Villa which was owned by the shipyard's manager, Adam Wood. In 1924 this was acquired by the District Welfare Committee as a convalescent home for miners' wives and daughters. (Miners themselves were given convalescent facilities at Kirkmichael Home near Maybole.) An extension was added to the house in 1936 and when Kirkmichael Home was closed twenty years later, the men were moved into the house which accommodated 24 men and 24 women until it also was closed.

Before the bathing pool opened in 1931, the youth of Troon went sea bathing off the rocks here at Betsy's Kirn at the end of Welbeck Crescent. Facilities included both a changing shelter and a springboard affixed to the rock. The area was still used for swimming in the 1950s even though by that time the deep water had silted up and the place was in general disrepair. In 1964 the *Troon & Prestwick Times* noted that it was probably named after a Betsy Miller, a well-known local character, who in the nineteenth century captained the brig *Clytus* whose home port was Saltcoats. This ship carried cargo down the Ayrshire coast and across to Ireland and it may have used the inlet for loading or unloading cargo.

Swimming Pond, Troon.

The Swimming Pond opened in 1931 and was always a popular venue in the summer months. Despite efforts to heat the water, the absence of a roof made its use seasonal and it was finally demolished in 1987 after the opening of the indoor pool.

The Rock Garden and the facade of the Swimming Pond. Despite the ravages of flooding from spring tides or during winter storms these gardens always recovered their distinctive look. The houses of Titchfield Road in the background are unchanged, although the site of the pool is now taken by a car park.

Portland Terrace, Titchfield Road and the Esplanade, pictured around 1906 – always a popular place to be seen walking out. Note the gangways on the sand for access to the boat hiring.

The bandstand was built in 1906 for entertaining the summer crowds and many top class and championship bands performed here before it was demolished in 1959.

THE BOATING POND, SEAFRONT, TROON.   A.619

The boating and paddling pond took the site of the bandstand after its demolition.

A young lad hard at work on his sand castle, *c.* 1910. The Old Parish Church, designed by Hippolyte Blanc, was built in 1894 and in 1975 the central spire had to be removed due to the effects of high winds and salt water damage. In the centre of the picture stands Marine Cottage, a private residence that was demolished in the early 1970s to make way for the luxury flats of Marine View Court.

THE ESPLANADE & BEACH, TROON.

A 1936 view over the golden sands of the South Shore towards Prestwick and Ayr. The small white hut in the centre at the foot of St Meddans Street was used to store deck chairs for hire while on the sand at the edge of the promenade stand two ice cream vending huts (the names Currie, Togneri and Ross's Dairy all come to mind). There are also two boat hirer's huts on the sand. At the time these probably belonged to Cuthill and McAuslan, although many may well remember another hirer, Johnny Warren, who took people to the Lady Isle on his boats the *Rose Marie* and the *Mary Anne*.

The putting green continues to be a popular summer attraction and a little putting practice before a game on one of the six local golf courses never goes wrong.

Ayr Street is unchanged today except for the demolition of the house on the left to make way for the Municipal Buildings and Concert Hall in 1932. The hall's stage facilities were the equal of many top theatres and there were a number of big names among those who trod the boards, including Jimmy Wallace, Robert Wilson, Chic Murray and Johnny Beattie, to name a few. The steeple is part of the original Old Parish Church (built in 1838) and the new Church was built alongside in 1894. On the opposite corner are premises occupied by the Royal Bank of Scotland (formerly the Commercial Bank) which were erected in 1900.

St Meddan's Street, *c.* 1905. At that time Portland Church had not yet been built and the steeple of St Meddan's Church (built in 1888) was without its clock which it later acquired from the demolished Portland Street U.F. Church in 1926. At the bottom of the street, the railway bridge was removed in the early 1970s.

The Bentinck Hotel was located on the corner of Bentinck Drive and St Meddan's Street and was possibly also known as Mar Lodge (the name on the building). This name was later given to a hotel in South Beach which has since been converted into flats.

A view of the top half of St Meddan's Street, taken from the railway bridge. On the extreme left is the Ardneil Hotel with its conservatory and the gable end of the former manse of St Meddan's Church. Ardneil Garage now occupies the ground behind the wooden fence where the trees are growing and to the rear of these properties lies the area called Low St Meddan's. The spire belongs to the Chapel of Our Lady of the Assumption and St Meddan which was built in 1911 to replace the chapel in Academy Street which had been established in 1883.

The bowling green and tennis courts off Bentinck Drive, pictured in 1952, are still in use today.

HARLING DRIVE TROON.

A view of Harling Drive looking north along the road bordering the Municipal Golf Courses. On some postcards the street name is given as 'Harlane' and apparently the original name was 'Harley', after the Duke of Portland's son. Around 1911 when Troon Town Council was taking over the roads from the feuars, the minutes were handwritten and the name may have been misread, resulting in its current form.

A view of the Municipal Golf Club House taken from the railway bridge at the station with the starter's box and Harling Drive behind. The three artillery guns parked in front were relics of the First World War.

MARR COLLEGE, TROON.

212804.J.V.

Charles Kerr Marr died in February 1919, leaving a bequest for the improvement of educational opportunities available in his home town. By the following year a school to accommodate 120 pupils was being planned by the Trustees but it wasn't until 1927 that they purchased Wallacefield Farm for use as its site. In 1930 a splendid new school had been completed at a cost of £238,000 and the property included a gate lodge, housewifery bungalow, sports pavilion and three masters' houses. Dr Alfred R. Murison was appointed rector in February 1930 but due to legal problems it was not until 4 September 1935 that the Marquis of Lothian declared Marr College open with a complement of 446 pupils.

All who attended Marr College will recall morning assembly which was held in the Concert Hall where the Rector usually gave a daily talk. Originally adjoining the hall were an art gallery and museum, but latterly demand for teaching space necessitated their conversion to classrooms. Note the footlights at the foot of the stage – when it was installed the hall's stage equipment was envied by many professional theatres of the day.

The Troon Old Course Golf Club was founded in 1878 on the lands of Craigend Farm. Initially it had only five holes, but was extended to twelve in 1883 and to eighteen three years later. The Championship Course, known for many years as Old Troon, has a notoriously difficult eighth hole known as the 'Postage Stamp', where former Open Champion Gene Sarazen had a hole-in-one in 1973. The sixth hole, at 577 yards, is the longest hole in the Open rota. The Ladies Championship was played there in 1904 and, beginning in 1923, the club has hosted six Open Championships with the most recent being in 1997. The club became Royal Troon in 1978 to mark its centenary and is the only one to be so honoured by the Queen. Its motto is *Tam Arte Quam Marte* – 'more by skill than effort' – which aptly sums up good golfing technique.

The Marine Hotel (now the Marine Highland) behind the club house was opened in 1895 and has provided superior accommodation to many notable visitors.

The Gyaws, Troon.

RELIABLE SERIES. K1739

These cottages, known as the Gyaws, were on the edge of Royal Troon course, towards the south end of Crosbie Road. The name derives from the old Scots word 'gaw', one of the meanings of which is a drain or hollow with running water in it.

This elegant thatched cottage was built in 1910 and stands at the entrance to Frognal House in South Woods, not far from the ruins of Crosbie Kirk.

This picturesque gate house for Fullarton House was known as the Heather House. It also stood within yards of Crosbie Kirk, but sadly it was destroyed by fire in 1958. The earliest mention of this church is from 1229 and there was once a hamlet clustered around it. The present ruins are of the second kirk which was built in 1681. On 25 January 1759, its roof was blown off and part of the gable wall collapsed during the same storm that heralded the birth of Robert Burns a few miles away in Alloway.

Old Row, Fullarton, Troon.

The cottages of Old Row on the Isle o' Pins Road belonged to the Fullarton estate. The unusual road name may have derived from the four pillars, or pins as they were called, that stood at the entrance to Fullarton House. A more fanciful explanation was given in an edition of the *Air Advertiser* from 1836 where mention is made of the Isle de Pinos, a small island off Cuba which was passed by ships plying the trading routes to and from the West Indies. The island may have been well-known to local sailors and it may have been that this scene reminded them of it. It is a thought!

Fullarton House was built by the Fullarton family in 1745 and stood sentinel as Troon developed from a few scattered houses to achieve Burgh status in 1896. In 1928 it was purchased by Troon Town Council and converted into flats, but by the 1960s the ravages of time had taken their toll on the building and the cost of modernisation could not be justified. It was razed to the ground in 1966. Some buildings at the southern end, erected in 1792 and used as stables and servants quarters, were rescued and converted to modern mews houses and the estate is now a park.

Loans Village lies two miles inland from Troon on what had been the turnpike road from Ayr to Irvine. Tam Fullarton is pictured standing outside the blacksmith business which had been in his family for many years. This has now been replaced by a petrol station. Some of the older houses in the village were probably used to hide smuggled contraband and in the nineteenth century pits were discovered beneath the floors of some buildings in which smuggled brandy had evidently been stored.

Barassie, which now lies within Troon Burgh boundaries, is believed to owe its beginnings to some Kilmarnock gentlemen who built a bowling green there so that they could play their favourite game while taking their families to the seaside. These houses were built on the north side of Barassie Burn around 1866 and were known as New Bank to distinguish them from the original group of eight cottages towards the centre of the picture called Old Bank.

On the north edge of the Clevance Hills (commonly known as the Dundonald Hills) and beside the road from Troon to Kilmarnock lies Hillhouse Quarry, owned by the Vernon family. When it opened in 1907 it produced 150 tonnes of stone per day and under continuing family ownership this has increased to the present 6,000 tonnes. This overview from the top of the finishing crusher shows how close the stone face was to the road and the reason for traffic being stopped during blasting.

These men, pictured around 1920, are preparing the stone face for blasting by drilling horizontally into the rock and packing explosives into the holes before detonation. The bogey track had to be manhandled out of the way before each blast to prevent rockfall damage.

Dundonald Castle

Archaeologists have discovered that the first castle at Dundonald (Donald's fort) was actually a Dark Age hill fort, although who Donald was is unknown. There was then a Norman motte and bailey and this was succeeded by a fortress type castle. The current building was erected around 1371 by Robert II, the first Stuart king, who used it as an occasional residence and died there in 1390. It later became the property of a succession of owners including the Cochrane family and lastly the Eglintons in the 1720s. By that time, however, it was already a ruin but it still provoked the interest of visitors – Boswell and Johnson visited in 1773. It remained as such until Historic Scotland acquired the site and after archeological research, the castle was officially opened as a visitor attraction and function hall in 1995.